Masked Identity

S. Marshall

AuthorHouse™
1663 Liberty Drive
Bloomington, IN 47403
www.authorhouse.com
Phone: 833-262-8899

Because of the dynamic nature of the Internet, any web addresses or links contained in this book may have changed since publication and may no longer be valid. The views expressed in this work are solely those of the author and do not necessarily reflect the views of the publisher, and the publisher hereby disclaims any responsibility for them.

Any people depicted in stock imagery provided by Getty Images are models, and such images are being used for illustrative purposes only.
Certain stock imagery © Getty Images.

This book is printed on acid-free paper.

ISBN: 978-1-6655-3510-6 (sc)
ISBN: 978-1-6655-3509-0 (e)

Library of Congress Control Number: 2021916613

Print information available on the last page.

Published by AuthorHouse 08/26/2021

authorHOUSE®

CONTENTS

PINK COMPASSION

FEMININE QUEEN

There is something about being a brown skin girl and we are taught to be independent and strong
Somehow to depend on others is seen as weak and wrong
It's like you have to be a superwoman with extraordinary powers to make it through
Because people look at you as weak, if anything can break you.
You have to be confident and at the same time possess femininity
Dress like a lady and be dainty
Cross your legs
Smile and be polite
Bow down gracefully
To prevent a fight
Never be unladylike

BEAUTY

When you try to define my beauty, you are putting a label on me
I have come too far to have one verb to completely describe me
My beauty shouldn't be question whether I am beautiful or not
I don't need anyone to categorize me as pretty, attractive, or hot
It's funny how someone opinions can affect the way a woman perceives herself
But I will not allow myself to be inferior to someone else
Beauty, what is it?
How can it be defined?
The definition has been expanded and changed over time
Every woman is beautiful no matter what race she may be
Never allow someone perception become your reality
Society has taught us that titles and labels
Give a person a sense of identity
I will not allow society
To define, create, or destroy me

BABY J

I look at you many days and my heart just melt
You lay your head upon my chest and it's the best feeling I evet felt
You look at me with your gray eyes and stare right into mine
When you hold your hand up to my chest, it makes me smile every time
No matter how I am feeling, you make me feel warm inside when you stare
I know I'm not the perfect mom but you make me feel like I'm the best there
When you stare at me, you look at me
As if I am the prettiest girl, you ever seen
You are my son and no one comes before you
You and I are a team!
You and I against the world
You mean the world to me
I love you Baby J
You are the best thing that has happen to me

CAN I

Can I get inside that mind of yours and allow it to be free?
Can you open up that wall you build and take a chance with me
Can you allow me to take you Places where you never thought you would go
Can I introduce you to a side of yourself that's more than physical
Can I show you I'm a woman to my word who is consistent and always maintain?
Can I introduce you to a chapter in your life title it's OK to change
Can I be the one you thought who only exist on tv
All I'm trying to get you to see it's OK to sample me
Can I be the reason those dimples always stay implanted on your face
Can I be the one your mind wonders off to when you're all alone in place
Let me be the one who you let in and show you more than I Can tell
Let me be the one who reaps the benefits of what true loves expels
When your back is up against the wall, allow me to lean towards you to give you a kiss
It's time to stop dreaming about it and come explore a love like this
Can I be the one?

ISN'T THIS POETIC

Isn't this poetic
How you show love and your sympathetic
Your love is authenticating, and I'm drawn to it like a magnetic
Your love is
Not artificial or synthetic
Being with you, isn't chaotic or hectic

This round I'm being selective
I want someone with style and ethics
So our love can be powerful, eccentric, and magnetic
Full of passion and energetic
A love that's overwhelmingly copacetic

CAN YOU

Can you love me past these scars I have accumulated over time
Can I trust you when you say your body is only mine.
Can you protect me from harm and vow to always tell me true?
Can I rely on you to show me a man honors what he says he will do.
Can you stimulate my mental and challenge me to always be my best.
Can I trust you would never put my loyalty to a test.
Can I count on you to always be there
Can I rely on you to always be fair
Can I consider you my friend when times get rough
Can I share my secrets with you and know you won't carry it away
I'm asking can I count on you to stay?

IF I TOLD YOU

If I told you, my primary mission is to make you mine
Would you try to fight me the entire time?
If I told you, my goal is to make sure the smile never leaves your face
Would you be willing to allow it to take place?
If I told you, I want to help you break free
Would you still bound yourself to captivity?

Peace, love and blessings

BLACK REFINEMENT

QUEEN

There is something about being a black woman that holds so much pride
A feeling that leaves you humble as well as satisfied
The feeling of knowing your overall being is the most copied and wanted traits
The kind of essences that's others cannot escape
Yes, it's true, your attitude can sometimes be thought of as an array of emotions
People are often intimidated because you don't break in the midst of commotion
Your style, your grace, your body, your shape
Are all admire for others to try to duplicate
Lots of women wonder about your power and beauty, and where it lies
Because the way you are built,
Full lip, big nose, wide hips and thick thighs
It makes others realize
Your melanin
Is a blessing
Everything about you is pure gold
Its so amazing just how your beauty unfolds

ARE U

Is peace with you
Or is it hell you are going through
Are you really happy?
Or letting time pass you?
Are you pursing your dreams?
Or are you going through the motions of life
Are you creating possibilities?
Or are you creating strife
Are you being all you can be
Or are your keeping the status quo
Have you acquired enough
Or are you going to continue to grow
Just let me know!

FIRED

Did anyone consider I have bills to pay
When they told me not to bother coming in the next day
Did anyone consider I have kids at home to feed
Who depends on my income to supply for their basic needs
Did anyone consider if I don't work
Then things don't happen
How do you expect me to create greatness?
If you are not giving me nothing
Did anyone consider I need a home to live
Did anyone bother to think of my kids when I was release form my job
Or thinking of my overall well being would have been too hard?
I'm just wondering when you made the decision to take my job away
Did you think of my responsibilities?
And the people I take care of with the money I make

GENERATIONAL CURSE

Trying so hard to avoid this family curse
Creating new actions to put this thing in reverse
Examining the ones who are already tainted and hurt
Vowing to myself to not get caught up in the hurt
Making the changes to allow my son and I to be free
Knowing I have the power to not allow negativity to seize
Just trying to create my own and in search of my own peace
Staying away from those who have a negative affect
Checking the ones who try to alter the positive effect
Benching players on the bench when trying to put thoughts in my mind
Being more selfish with who gets my energy and time

HAVE YOU EVER

Have you ever had to look your daughter in the eye and not be able to feed?
Have you ever had to have sex with someone just to be able to meet your basic needs?
Have your ever felt like things in your life could be better
Have you ever sat back and plan how you can get your life together?
Have you ever looked across the table at the person you were with and said this will not last long?
Have you ever did right by someone who did you wrong?
Have you ever been so broken you have no sense of direction to go?
The people who said they would have your back isn't there anymore
Have you ever thought to yourself you might be losing your mind?
Have you ever thought you could but procrastinate because you thought you had time?

HONOR

We honor you black man and all that you do
If anyone hasn't told you, we love and respect you
From the way you make things happen, when it seems like there is no way at all
From the way you get things done when our children seem to call
I cherish you and love you
In every way I can
I know life is hard for you
Being a superior man

I CAN TEACH MY SON

I can teach my son "I'm black and proud"
But don't say it too loud
I can teach my son to make his own way and don't follow the crowd

I can teach my son his race is superior, and he is the greater man
But in a matter of seconds his life can be taken away because he is a COLORED MAN

I can teach my son to raise his hand up high and yell don't shoot
I cant help him if someone is racist or fearful
And decide to enforce him to be mute.

I can teach my son his rights and allow him to recite them once more
Society will teach him what it means to be a black man and what to look out for

I can teach him not to be fearful
Always do the right thing
Just make sure you are teaching your children
The same exact thing

I can teach him not to disrespect the law and always follow their directives
Even though they may do something to you and be disrespectful
I can teach my son to follow the law and not be apprehensive
But his blackness may come across as too proud and too offensive

I can teach my son he may be smarter and even better, but he will have to work extra hard
To always be prepared and never lower his guard
I can teach my son everything and prepare him for his truth
Unfortunately, I cannot teach him how to change the mind set of the racist people too.

I RECEIVED FLOWERS TODAY

I received flowers today
After our horrible fight
Filled with empty promises
Of how I will be treated right

I received flowers today
Serenade with a ballad of a love song
Telling me how much you love me
And you will never do me wrong
I recd flowers today
Sealed with a kiss
Filled with I'm sorry
And I will never hurt you again like this

I received flowers today
Not because I'm special
Or a gesture of love
It's because the bruise on my shoulders
From the ground when was shove

I received flowers today
Along with other grand gestures
Telling me how I am loved
And one of his best treasures

I received flowers today
Not for just being me
I received flowers today
So I can let the past be.

SINGLE BLACK FEMALE

I often here people say black women are
Underrated
Hated
Complicated
Appreciated
Violated
Intimidating
Domesticated
Unsaturated
Fabricated
Dedicated
Captivating
Ameliorated
Elaborated
Yes, we are all of that but don't forget educated!

THANK YOU

I want to say thank you
To every rejection
Every denial that came my way
Thank you for the failed opportunities
That could not stay
Thank you for the lies
All the plots and schemes
Thank you for showing me
Jealously can be a fiend
Thank you for the talk abouts
The doubts and all the pain
Pressure bust pipes
Watch how I sub to this change

YELLOW ROSE

SURVIVOR QUEEN

Feet planted to the ground
Don't know which way to start
This thing called life
Has left me emotionally scarred
Back up against the wall
Don't want to ask for help
Cause every time I do
People ask why I can't do it myself
Hard to turn to love ones
when things are not going right.
I know I wasn't build to give up
so easily on a fight.
Struggling to make the ends meet
not enough to make do
I'm fighting this battle and
I am lost about what to do
Just when I thought it was over and thought it was all done
Things would start to change and
I would remember I'm not done
Things were getting brighter
I could see things clear,
I had to learn to let go and conquer my own fear,
Now things are finally starting to turn around
I knew I wasn't built to remain down
Some enemies thought they had won
Some enemies thought they would see
Not knowing the survivor and fighter I have within me
I almost gave up and threw the towel in
Then thought about my kids and knew failure was not an option
I had to win!

TRUE HAPPINESS

True happiness is amidst
I'm excited about this
Time to conquer the world
So my fears I dismiss
Surrounding myself by greatness
Is what my future consist
Evaluating my life
And checking off my list
Remembering the days
I prayed about this

I NEVER KNEW

I never knew I was so strong until I stopped being weak
I never knew I had a voice until I heard myself speak
I never knew I could until I found out I can
I never knew that being alone is good until I found myself without a man
I never knew feelings until I felt
I never knew some words could cause your heart to melt
I never knew pain until it was dealt
I never knew me until I got to know myself
I never knew heartache could be such a great deal
I never knew that some people are fake
until I starting hanging with people who was real
I never knew how good it felt to be alone
I never knew how bad things were until I saw all the wrong

OPEN HAND

Guard up
Even though he is about to fall
Told him last time
One call that's all
She screwed him over
He said it won't happen again
So even though he want it
He's like no we better as friends

Different chick's chasing
Which keeps the mind racing
And even though he isn't like other dudes
His act is slow pacing

Pacing

There are women out there
offering to pay for his time
He is not choosing any of them
one unicorn at a time
To be in his submission is a competition
They are all on his tail
He knows what he wants
So he just smile and wish them well

DO YOU SEE

The happiness of freedom
I display in my face
Do you see the joy I have
Knowing I travel at my own pace
Do u see my eyes
As if I have stars glowing from my eyes
Do you See

SELFISH

I'm going to be selfish this time
I'm going to only focus on me
I'm not trying to be rude
Just going to take the time out for me
I'm going to be selfish with my time
I'm going to be selfish with my space
I want to know the energy surrounded by me
Is meant to be in my space.
I'm not going to fall for the I love u
Or the good sex one may achieve
I need to know without a shadow of doubt
This person is meant for me.

GIVE

I give so much of me to others
I don't have anything left to give.
I been so busy doing for others
My life I have forgotten to live.
I have been many things to many people
I have played different roles
It's time for me to take over
And take control
I don't mind giving
But I have to give some to myself
I can't depend on anyone
I have to make a way for myself

FEEL

Its important to feel
So you can heal
Anything left covered
Goes un heal
Don't conceal
Your bruises or pain
Work on healing
So your life can change
Let it all out
So you can be free
Heal from your past
So you can find peace

BOTTLE OF WINE

A bottle of wine
Makes everything fine
Gives you a chance
To relax and unwind
Grab a bottle
And plan out your day

GREEN PROSPERITY

SERENITY QUEEN

It's something about being a black woman
that often goes underrated.
Even by our own people
we are often under value and not appreciate.
Often ridicule for our looks, size and shape,
Then criticize by other women for the things we intake
We are all fighting battles
some big and some are small.
Serenity to all my queens
Prosperity to you all.

UNTAMED

I don't want to play that role anymore.
I will let my hair go untame.
I shouldn't have to conform
for someone to remember my name.
My hair doesn't have to be sleek or long,
In fact, I like it bushy and wild.
Dreaded up or flared up
Is my personal style.

MENTAL STIMULATION

U say u prefer someone to provide you with mental stimulation.
How about I finesse you with my words and provide u oral stimulation
But not relation

I'm talking about the type of stimulation which will allow you to prosper and grow
The kind were you aspire to be and do so much more
I'm offering to take u on a different type high
One were you don't have to rely on an artificial supply
I want to balance out your charkas
and get you align
Have you feeling refresh and rejuvenate while I integrate your mind
Allow me to stimulate your mental and exercise your right to be free
Are you ready to explore this mental stimulation with me?

TODAY

Today I cried a river
I cried to there was nothing left
I thought about harming me
But had already done enough harm to myself

Today I died mentally
And decided to bury the past
I wanted more out of life
And decided suffrage couldn't last
Today I cried far the little girl

Who never received justice for herself

Today I decided
I had to look out for me
I couldn't keep depending on anyone else
Today I buried my sorrow, my hate and all my pain.
I decided if I wanted to be free

Then obviously some things had to change

Today I cried a river
As I watched it overflow
To love and hate your self
Leaves no room for personal growth.
Today I accepted me
All the pain all the hurt
CONSOLE BY FORGIVENESS
I cried from a simple touch.

FINALLY

Finally able to get in the bed after a long day.
Just want to relax in my night gown and in the bed I lay.
As I plan out my week to come
U know the bills, my outfits, and food.
I reflect on my day
As I almost lost my cool
It's hard remaining professional
U have to bite your tongue and remain humble.
U have to keep reminding yourself
Not to join the circus or the jungle.
When u reflect back on the things u got to loose
U realize u have to always have things together
Don't allow anyone to come and ruffle your feathers
So as I relax on this cozy night
Wrap in a blanket on the sofa
I'm just happy to be home
And all the none sense is over

LITTLE GIRL IN ME

I couldn't afford to be that little girl anymore because she didn't get any results.
All she was good for was a good laugh, selfies, and insults.
I knew I had to do better because there was so much I wanted to achieve
But the little girl in me would hold me back because she was naive
All I ever wanted was a level of great success
But the little girl in me was such a hot mess
I knew I had to make changes but something was holding me back
But the little girl in me couldn't acknowledge what we lack
Prefect patty she pretend to be
the little girl could never admit to any mistakes
The grown woman in me was willing to admit
of all the wrongs we make.
And both of us had a dire need of wanting to do better
We knew we couldn't co-exist in this world together.
So we had to decide if we were going to be successful
which person we wanted the world to see.
I decided to be successful
It was time to let go of the little girl inside of me.

VOW

I vowed to never hurt again
Never make the same mistake
I vowed to always be confident in every decision I make.

I vowed to never give up and always stand tall
I vowed even though I may stumble just remember to not to fall

I vowed to give it my all and always do my very best.
I vowed to always be prepared
For every lesson and every test

I vowed to never allow myself to be caught up again
I vowed to be a better mother, lover, and friend,

NATURE

Staring out into nature
AS I listen to the bird calls
Looking out my window
As I watch the leaves fall
Listening to the rain
As it hit the window pane
Seeing the symbolism
Confirmation of a change
Enjoying the wind howls
As it calls out to me
Reminding me to secure happiness
And be all I can be

RENEWED

Come celebrate with me and the changes I made
Come celebrate with me and the second chance I was gave

Let me tell you how

I had to pray myself out of misfortune,
No guidance or reassurance for this little orphan

Nobody ever was there to show me the way.
Everything I earned I had to make a way

I had to let go of my troubling past
I asked for God to deliver me and I was recast

WOMAN IN THE MIRROR

There were times I felt like giving up
but look back and saw who was looking in the mirror
On my darkest days you made
the vision seem much clearer
I always want u to know
everything I do I try to give it my best
Because I know from you
You won't accept anything less

GRUDGE

It took me a moment to get passed all the hurt and pain
I remember day in and day out praying for things to change
I remember holding on to things because I didn't want to let it go
Guess that was my way of trying to gain some control
Due to me not being able to control all the negative things that happen
I put up a facade and pretend I was affected by nothing,
It's something about being a black woman and being raise to believe we have to
be strong
Maybe that's why so many of us hold on to things for so long.
I had to unlearn the things that was keeping me behind
It's like I was repeating the same battles that held my family back time after
time.

WINE DOWN

After a long days of work
I return home
Immediately removing my bra
And relaxing to my favorite song
With a glass of wine in one hand
The remote in the other
Then the phone rings
Its a call from my mother
We laugh we joke
Reminisce about our day
We end the phone call
By saying be mindful of what u say
And I resume my liberation
Of the moment of being free
Free from the world
Free from insecurity,
My mind begins to explore
Alternative endings of my day
As I prop my legs up
To reflect upon my day
I grab my glass of wine
To reflect on the things people did and what they had to say,

BROWN SHADE

RELIABLE QUEEN

Hey girl
Just want you to know you got this,
Don't worry,
don't fret,
just go in with a clear heart and mind and do it.
Know for every action is a reaction.
Remember when you complete this chapter of your life make sure you never open
it again. Also remember during these times faces were revealed. It Hurts right
now but time will definitely heal this wound.
In the meantime, focus on you and your son and how u will provide a better
tomorrow for you guys.

As always peace, love and blessings

WHAT IS IT

What is it about your happiness that u don't want to choose
Are you afraid you won't be successful or are you afraid you will lose?
Are you afraid others won't like it and won't view it as a success
Are you afraid your efforts won't be viewed as your best?
What is it that keeps you
From giving it your all
Are you afraid

MISUNDERSTOOD

I'm studying your moves and I hear them loud and clear.
Even though we are not speaking, your voice keeps ringing in my ear.
I'm not going to classify u as a fuck boy but just a boy who is use to getting what
He likes
So pardon me if my next phrase seems impolite.
Yes, I want u but I'm not about to pay for your time
Not when you have other women waiting in line
I see u play on my vulnerabilities because u know how much I want u.
Little do you know if not reciprocated, I grow to not need you.
Just to let u know I'm close to walking out the door for good.
I'm tired of my feelings being taken for granted and misunderstood

BROKEN GIRL

I saw this beautiful girl
Who had been broken
Searching for acceptance
So she buy people with tokens
She had a kind heart
But had suffered a lot of pain
All the negativity that surrounds her
Made it hard for her to change
Scatter pieces
Made it hard to put them back together
She would go on and suffer
In the misery forever

MENTALLY DRAINED

I was drowning and it was like I was caught in a nightmare
If anyone would have tried to get close, I would caution like, BEWARE
I was mentally drained and physically weak
I had so much to say but didn't have the words to speak
Bills were stack so high they were greeting me at the door
I had to scrape up pennies one time I went to the store
Sometimes I had less than 40 to my name
I was drowning in debt yet still trying to maintain,
Maintain this lifestyle I built before it all came crashing down
I had reached my lowest and I was lost in the lost and found.
I was tired both physically and mentally drained
I had drown my sorrow in alcohol to mask the pain
But nothing change
Just more so the same thing

BURIED TREASURE

Hidden was a jewel stored in a case
Often misunderstood sometimes out of place
Often taken for granted and placed in the wrong hands.
Life had a way of showing her not to put trust in any man
Many has tried to tame her and take away her pride
No one knew the jewel, which was held inside.
Locked and buried so deep was a jewel who yet to arise.
Kept hidden for so long, when it surface, it was a surprise.

DISTANCE

The thing about distance is
it leaves two people apart
Make u question
do u really have their heart,
I mean how can u love someone and intentionally hurt
Cant live separate lives
thinking things will work

The thing about being distant
U have to want to go there
You have to be willing to put in work
To show the person you care

EVER

Ever been with a crowd of people but feel all alone.
Ever felt like the people you are with are strangers in your home.
Ever contemplated your next move but decide to move out the way.
Ever type a whole paragraph then delete every word u wanted to say.
Ever been so angry all you could do was cry
Ever told someone the truth but they prefer the lie.

LADY WITH THE BLUES

LOYAL QUEEN

Bag Lady
That's too many bags you carry
These bags are the reason you can never be merry
Walking around with the weight of the world on your shoulder
Each disappointment has made your heart colder
The disappointments has weighed you down and destroy your happiness in return.
Its ok, fix your crown, those were lesson you had to learn.

EVERY TIME

Every time I took you back thinking you were going to change
I cant be mad at you for coming back and serving me the same thing.
You would whisper your sweet notes and sang your soft praises in my ear
Yet every time you would come back by you would bring back a new fear.
Your inconsistency taught me just how selfish people could be with your time
It also taught me how inconsiderate I was with mine
It's like every time 1 tried over and over again to let you back in
The more I realize I am fighting a losing battle, I would never win
It's because of your inconsistent ways I saw the contradiction within myself
I can't proclaim self love if I allow mistreatment from someone else

I WAS IN LOVE

I was in love with someone who didn't love me.
I gave him my all to see how unselfish I could be.
I was in love with someone who was taking complete advantage of me
While I was building us a future, he was destroying our family

I gave him my all and I gave him my last.
In return all he would do is show his ass.

NEW U

He would make me question everything about myself and the person I am
He made me second guess the pictures and avoid all the cams
He would take me through the highs and bring me to my lows
But he always soften it with a kiss with each and every blow
He would make me second guess myself and everything I wanted to be
He would make me lose faith and question how I really feel about me.
Yet he would make me want him all the while
He would be the reason I would frown and be the reason why I smile
What's funny the more pain he caused, the more I drew to
He would be the reason why I moved on because I couldn't trust the old you.

COMFORT ME WITH LIES

The list of questions I would ask him the answers never came
He would give me every reason to love him and every reason for it to change
He would make me love him and commit suicide with his lies
He wanted all of me but my dignity I could not compromise
He would feed me with the empty promises and try to comfort me with the lies he told.
Hidden agendas and many lies was often sold
He would manipulate with his words and destroy me with his actions
Then pretend he was innocent and he did nothing.

REJECTED

For some odd reason I loved this man even though he offered me nothing in life.
I mean time and time again he proved to me there will always be strife.
I would call him and text him my calls got rejected
My feelings I poured out to him but I was never the one he elected.
I loved him on purpose and I was willing to give him my all
He only offered me detachment and occasional booty calls
It's funny because the more time spent
I came to realize that this would never be
I don't know why I wanted him and he never was willing to choose me.

DON'T

Dont tell me you love me then turn around and hurt me again.
Don't allow me to get attached and then tell me later we better off being as friends.
Don't allow me to feel if you know u really don't care.
Don't talk about feelings which you know u don't share.
Don't make love to me and having me falling so deep.
Don't disappear from me before I fall asleep.
Don't abandon me whenever I need you the most.
Don't say give it time if you never plan for it to grow.
Don't deceive me with all those misconceptions.
Don't have me traveling down a road without a sense of direction.

Don't♤

SUMMERTIME

It's something about the summer which makes him distant and me more confuse.
It's like we are on a good path then he vanishes without any clues
I reach, I try, but it is hard to get him back in
I think, this go around, what he does, he will win.
I don't have the energy to convince and try to convey.
I can't make you love me and I can't make u stay.

IF I

If I give it to you, would you promise to keep it protected.
If told you I have a hard time trusting people, would you be able to respect it.
If I give you the one thing, I never been able to give before.
Would you be receptive or find it difficult?
If I told you all my secrets, share with you what makes me hurt.
If I go against my instincts and decide to put u first.
Will you be able to carefully handle or dismantle such a precious gift?
Or would it be destroyed by the possibilities of what if.
I want to know if I give u this one thing which can cause so much despair.
Would you promise to keep it safe and free from repair?

ALL MY EX STUFF

I packed all my ex stuff
And put it in a box to throw away
They had already held
Too much time and too much space.
I had held on to the items
For so many years and so long.
I couldn't go another year
Housing them in my home
I had went thru my phone
Deleted all the messages too
I decided this was your last year
Occupying that space too
I took all the pictures
Set fire to the furnace
Watching the burning flame
Was all I need for affirmance
Every item, every gift
I packed it up to give away,
Those things are no longer welcome
Like you, it can not stay.

ORANGE DELIGHT

FLAMBOYANT QUEEN

Dear beautiful queen
Do you know how beautiful u are
Don't let people make you think, you take things too far
Be proud
Be loud
Live free
Unapologetically
Be you
Do you
Do whatever makes u happy
Be selfish with your time
Apologize for nothing
Do self-care
Establish financial health
Do whatever u need to be free
Embrace the beauty of yourself
For the color girls like me

OPINIONS, LABELS AND ROLES

I'm strong but don't take my crying as weak
Don't say I have an attitude because sometimes I don't speak.
When I voice my opinion don't label me as rude.
When I walk away from others don't say I'm being cruel
Don't put labels on me when I defend myself
Don't try to compare me to anyone else
Don't box me in because I don't do well in a cage
Don't say I practice voodoo because I utilize my sage
Don't based your opinions, your labels, your roles, or definitions on me
I don't have to cross my legs or wear a dress to be considered a lady.
If I choose to go braless, its because I want to be free

FEEL LIKE

Feel like I been cage for a while and didn't have any room to grow
Everyone was making progress
but mine was kinda slow
Its like I was stuck in a stage where things were constantly remaining the
same.
I knew I could not remain here, things had to make a drastic change

CLOSET

I'm not in the closet
I don't choose to hide
It's just certain things I keep private
Out of respect for my children pride

I'm not in the closet
I live my true
It's just certain aspects
I wish not to disclose to you

I'm not in the closet
It's out on display
Its true happiness
It does not have to be announced in any way

See I'm not in the closet
There are certain things I dont want mishandle
I see what the world could do
Leave you shatter and dismantle

SEARCHING

I'm searching for the meaning of life
Where it seems to remain conceal
I have some wounds and overtime they still have not heal
And I dont feel
Not the way society wants me to feel
But I feel oppression
The things THAT have came my way
has made me numb
Even at my lowest
I manage to not feel
Suffering from an alertness
Of managing how to deal
Though my head hangs low
Where it was once high
The days may get dark but I get up and try
I press on like there is nothing left
I decided to have something to give
Even if it means forgiving myself

GIRLS NIGHT OUT

I want to gather all my friends and we sit back and drink wine
I want us to sit back and relax as we all recall the different times
The times we laughed, we cried, and felt despair
A moment of weakness is what I want us to share.
I want us to uplift each other and sing each other different praises
I want us to laugh as we all share how we make it throughout the day.
Let's get together and put on our sexist clothes and make up on
Let's get together to talk about our weakness and what makes us strong
Let's get together and plan a special event
Let's get together and boast about how we are all angel sent
Let's get together and take many selfies throughout the night.
Toast a few bottle of champagne as we celebrate the good life.
Let's get together and celebrate the accomplishments we all have made
Let's get together and recall the things we did and the roads we pave.
Let's get together to discuss our next steps and goals
Let's get together before we are wrinkle and too old.

I CRIED MY LAST TEAR

I cried my last tear
Cried until nothing was left
Thought some negative thoughts
Thought about giving up on myself
How did I get here
Which turn was to many lefts
Now I'm left all alone
Trying to figure it out for myself
I Cried a bucket of tears
In my tears, I drown
I search for peace
To no avail none was found
Surrounded by silence my thoughts are speaking so loud
It's like my life is consume
ROUND this deep dark cloud
I have cried all the tears
Cried until there was nothing left
I cried and I cried
Until the tears filled the shelf

IF I TOLD YOU

If I told u, you are beautiful
You probably wouldn't believe I am telling the truth,
If I say your look is captivating
You would swear 1 was running game on you.
If I told u I had your best interest in heart, and I just want to see you grow
If I told u I admire u
You would swear I was putting on a show
If I told I was willing to invest in your dreams
And by helping u with yours isnt a hindrance with mine,
U would swear I had a hidden agenda by giving u some of my time
If I told u, all I want is for u to be happy.
U would swear people just dont say or do anything for nothing
If I told u I want u to be the best you can and hope u succeed.
U would swear it must be something in it for me.
If I told you, Queen, I am here to protect your throne.
You would question it and automatically try to find something wrong.

SEARCHING FOR

In the midst of my success, I search for the ones I admired the most
Some are not famous like my favorite tv host.
I'm talking about the women who get up everyday to go to work.
Working seven days a week, being a mother, spouse, and attending church.
The people who when I was feeling low encourage me to do right
The people who wasn't there physically but their vision was always in sight
I salute you all for standing in your Truth
Correcting me and defending me even when I didn't know what to do.
For the moments I felt low, you encourage me to fly high
Even at my lowest, you were beside me when I wanted to cry
I salute all the beautiful women who are mighty and strong
Even if u are not right, no one can convince me you are wrong

DEAR BIG GIRL

Got some extra fat around my waist guess u can call it extra cushion.
Just a little something extra for him to grab on when he is doing his pushing.
Don't come at me talking bout I need to loose some weight.
My face and smile alone makes a skinny girl hate.
Big breast and well rounded, guess you can say I am extra bless.
Don't think for one second this lady don't get test.
And if u are confuse let me simplify it for u.
Don't think for one second your man wont try me too.
No, I don't have a problem with my weight I love the skin I'm in.
U trying to do extra things to get this thicken.
So no I don't compare myself to u or wish I was smaller.
I dont have to do all those extra things to gain a few followers.

INVITE

Guess I wasn't popular enough to get the invite.
Must didn't have the proper shade, weight or height.
I guess I wasn't appeasing to the eye.
Or perhaps its because I don't embellish in a lie
Not being invited let's you know where you stand
Be careful not to trust every person smile and hand
Some people don't have the right intention.
Especially when it comes to inviting and your name is not mention.
Guess my energy wasn't meant to sit at the table.
All energy cant afford to surrounded by fables.

NEW FOUNDATION

As I embrace this new foundation
I have laid down in life
I'm hoping this year will bring me prosperity as I ignore the strife
I will walk this path of righteous
With my head lifted high
Knowing all my goals will be accomplish
Because the limit is within the sky.
As I embark on this journey
I promise to always speak the truth
I hope to be able to empower and lift others
With my wisdom and words of truth
As I continue to walk this path
I watch all the walls crumble down
This year I promise to never
Let diamonds fall from my crown.

GIRL WITH UNWONTED NAME

This is for the little girl with the unwonted name.
Who name had to be shorten for others or change
The little girl with the long name and vibrant personality to match.
The one who is often considered based on her name she isn't tact.
For the Quilas, Nika Yika, Drikas and Nesha
The person who is often judge by their looks and their features
Wear you name proud
Don't allow anyone to make u feel ashamed
Know that your name is beautifully created
Everyone doesn't have the honor of an unique name
Next time someone says your name and gets it wrong
Stand tall and look them in their eyes
Say it proud and say it strong
Let them know your name deserves some respect
Just like your name, make it an experience they wont forget.

PURPLE MELODY

PEACEFUL QUEEN

At this place called peace, everything seems to be going well.
Thankful for the times even when I was going through hell
Happy about this place I currently reside
Not allowing anything to steal my joy and pride
At this place, I begin to heal
At this place, I begin to feel
In touch with the past and embracing the future
Happiness is aboard and I'm excited about what to do with you

CROSSROADS

Forever at a crossroads
About which direction to go
Lost of faith
And lost of hope
Wanting so much
Yet feeling so overwhelm
Wanting to confide in others
But afraid of being condemned
Trying to find a way
To ensure I am always eating
Negative remarks
I am always defeating
I am trying to walk down a path
Where I can flourish and grow
Making bad decisions
Is not an option anymore.

HIDDEN ROSE

Hidden and buried under a rock
Found on the corner or the end of the block
Is a rose fighting to make its way through
May have been stumped on by a few shoes
But still it prevails making it way and taking a stance
Even though no none is nurturing it and giving it a chance
It remains apprehend
As it continues to sprout through
Always conquering and not forgetting it's roots

FREE

Dancing in the rain and I feel free
No amount debt
Will suffocate me
Vibing to the music
As I sit all alone
Strolling through my apps
As I ignore the calls coming through my phone
Planning ahead
So I can accomplish all I need
This go around
I'm going to be selfish with all of me

TOUCH

I don't know what it is about your touch that has me so weak.
It's like when your hands met my body it made it difficult for me to speak
I wanted you and craved u in every way possible
When I'm with u, I feel like I can accomplish the impossible
Is it true, we all yearn for what the heart desires
It's something about your touch which sets me on fire
I love u and love kissing on your neck
The way you embraces me in your arm shows my body the much needed respect
Your touch has the way of eating away my pain
And when you caress my body things are never the same
I love u and u love me
apparently I love the way
Your touch soothes me.

WOULD BE DAD

All I ever wanted was for my son to have a dad, he could be proud of
Someone he could turn to and offer him guidance, protection, and love
His own personal hero who would be there and teach him life lessons
Someone to play catch, ride bikes, and four wheelers
Who would teach him to not do drugs and chase away the drug dealers
I wanted my son to have the one thing…. The one thing I never had
That was someone he could call…..that someone
would be DAD.

PLAY MY ROLE

I can only do my part
even though the role is small.
Sometimes people can push u to the limit
where u willing to risk it all.
Sometimes I feel like I'm in a place, where I am out of place, and things won't
change
Sometimes I feel like why bother
they want it to remain the same.

FOOD MOOD

One of the toughest battles I had to fight was my relationship with food.
Everyday I would wake and eat whatever depending on my mood.
Finding a reason to celebrate any occasion just to eat.
Always the first and the last to leave the seat.
I watched as the weight piled up and each time saying I'm going to do better.
Making weight goals saying this will not last forever.
What I have discover through this quest, is the food journey has to end
I'm fighting for my health this season has just begin

UNPLUG

Nights like this when we are all alone
Sipping on wine and unplugging from our phones
Cuddling up with you brings me so much peace
When I'm with you, all my negative thoughts seize
It's funny I never thought I would feel this way
Until our paths cross and we met that day
Each day with you our love grows stronger
Nights like this, I wish could last much longer.
When we lock lips and kiss
Its times like this
I never want to miss

HEAVY LIES THE HEAD

Heavy lies the head while people attack THE crown
Some people try to throw me under, but I wasn't built the drown.
They see me with this smile and want to see my frown.
They thirsty for attention but I offer them no sound.

Heavy lies the head while people playing with my mental.
Instead of responding to THE negativity
I focus on my temper.
Working on my brand so I can build my empire.
The little attention I gave to some people is now due to expire.
Fake friends coming towards me trying to drill in and inquire
Current situations, I'm trying to explore my priors
People get offended by the look of my attire.
Little ones look up to me and tell me they admire.
Others tell me, my story inspires

Leaches coming at me in all kind of directions
Secret lives and public lies is what I'm detecting
Trying to craft my moves is what I'm perfecting,
Guards up, so beware, the crown is what I'm protecting.

RED PASSION

NUBIAN WARRIOR QUEEN

Its something about being a black woman that imposes a certain level of threat.
How battles are often fought demanding equality and respect.
People call you angry or bitter when u put them in check.

I WISH I HAD MY DAD

I wish I had my dad
I wish I could see his face
I wish I knew the truth
Of that night u fought your last race
I wish I could talk to him
Let him know the pain I feel
I wish this was a nightmare I wish this wasn't real
I wish I could attend the father and daughter dance
As u sit me down and caution me of my wrongs
I wish just for one moment
You could visit my home
I wish I had my dad
So he can wrap me in his arm
Kiss me on my forehead
And keep me safe from harm
I wish I had my dad
To confide in about My doubts
Chase away the people
Who cause confusion in my house
I wish I had my dad so I can recd a hug to drown my problems away
I wish I had my dad who would know just what to say
I wish I had my dad

WORDS

Wounds can heal so fast, wounds can heal so slow
 Its up to you do you hold on tight or let it go
Even though healing is hard, you have to heal in order to grow
Holding on to something will allow your offender to win once more
Words are the most powerful weapon, it cuts through you and leave such an ugly scar
Some words can really define just how heinous or beautiful people are
Words can be so deadly and can bust your heart as it cut through you like a knife
It can enhance, scar, or ruin your life
Most people don't realize the damage words can cost
Words can lead you or cost you to be lost
Words are like fire they can burn a whole into your heart
Words can cost people to stay or even fall apart
Words can affect the body even worst damage the soul
It's up to you rather you let the wound expand or take control
Words can spread over your body like a ruthless disease
Words can destroy you or put your pain at ease
People say sticks and stones may break my bone but wards will never hurt me
But let me be earnest
Words do hurt they can burn like fire in a furnace

TRUST

He had the type of eyes that were always so convincing.
Sitting here right now as I keep reminiscing.
Time and time again I kept telling myself
Its me he wants and he doesn't need anyone else
He had me so convince THAT I was the only one he loved and desired.
But those frequent like buttons were often hit for others he admired.
Even though he told me over and over again, I was the only person he wanted
and need
He still find ways to give others his forbidden seeds
He took something from me I can never get back
No matter how hard I try I couldn't forget the fact.
I loved him, trust him, and would have gave him my all.
Yet still he was out there willing to risk it all

ANGER

I'm so angry with myself
I have so much anger held inside
I know I need to forgive myself
But this feeling I can't hide
Feel like I'm paying
For a mistake made so long ago
Holding on to the past
Prevents me from moving forward

CRAVE

U don't understand because I don't understand it either
It's like I crave your touch.
When you're not around, I miss you so much.
Every day you are on my mind
I be wanting to give you my spare time.
Constantly thinking of ways to please.
Ways to bring your stress life to an ease.
Willing to do what I can for you.
Just want to let u know how much I love you.
See you bring out the poetry in me.
U have no idea of how much u inspires me.
From the way you walk, the way you talk.
Your little bit of curly hair.
It's something about you that makes me go there.

VIBE

How about we sit back and relax, and I expose you to a side you didn't know
exist.
As we lay back and discuss some things we avoid and dismiss.
We vibe to the music as Silk and Dru Hill guide our way.
We lay in each other arms and let the music say the words we don't say.
As we lay here naked, exposing ourselves in a different view.
Let's mentally fuck each other as we explore this inner view.

MY OWN KARMA

Was it My own karma
Staring me in my face
Was it the payback
For the things that took place
Was I being force to now accept consequences for my actions
Has the time come
For me to stop reacting

I DON'T WANT TO FEEL LOVE

I don't want to feel love
Especially if it's going to hurt
I whether remain single
Because I know my worth
I don't want to hear u say u love me
If you are into playing games
I don't have time to interact
If you are into playing games
I don't want to hear you say u love me
Then use that same mouth to tell me lies,
I would rather u be up front with me
So I'm aware of where my future lies
I don't want to give my all
Then in return receive nothing
I whether continue to live this life I live
Enjoy all that is happening

I LOVE ME

I look in the mirror and see some things has change
After all these years, things don't appear the same.
What was once tight and fit is now loose and jiggles.
Not to mention I have extra cushion in the middle
When I look in the mirror, I see change and growth,
I see a woman who voice her concerns vs the little girl who never spoke.
I see growth spiritually, mentally, physically, emotionally as well.
When I look in the mirror I can see myself.
I love the person who I have decided to be
I love her for who she is
I love me

HURT AGAIN

I held on to so much hurt
Because I thought u did me wrong
Because in the moment I needed u
You chose weakness instead of being strong.
I allowed the hurt and anger
Lead me down a path of great mistakes
I allowed that anger
To fuel and grow to a passion of hate
I didn't realize that the hate I was given u
Was completing destroying me
Guess it's true when people say
Hate loves misery
So I forgive you for the pain
And I hope u can do the same
Though I know we can't have a do over
But this pattern of hate I wish to change.
As I forgive u for your wrong doing
I have chose to forgive myself
Because mentally I am drowning
And I want to save myself

LOSS AND MISTAKES

I had taken all the losses one person could ever take.
I knew my next move was my best move
I couldn't bare anymore mistakes.
I had failed over and over again then I hit a new level of low,
I was at the bottom of the pit
I didn't have anymore room to grow
every night I would pray for a breakthrough
Asking God over and over again
Would HE guide me and protect me and when was my season to win
I had crash, lost everything that once meant the world to me.
I dont ever want to lose again
I'm on a winning spree

MS. USA

needs glasses and so does the justice system too.

How does one expect someone to be rehabilitated but can't find any work to do?

People looking at them different when they check the box stating they have been arrested before.

Cant get a decent job only at a fast food or grocery store.

It seems, help only comes to a single mother and child.

Leaving the men to fiend from the wicked and wild.

Ms. USA is willing to help if your income falls below a certain level,

I thought this was the land of the free why the lower income gets group together.

Dont mean to ruffle feathers

But it seems, the goal is for the poor to remain broke,

Just so you are able to recd the government support.

It's like there is no hope for the middle class to receive any help.

If you are middle class, you have to do it all by yourself.

That's why I say Ms. USA needs glasses so she can see the so called land of the free.

Is not design to support people of color like you and me.

The justice system needs glasses because once you are out and try to reform.

It's like a stamp of "I been to prison before" is constantly worn.

People are being denied jobs based on their past.

Yet get criticize if they were to sit at home on their ass.

DOUBT

Everyday I wake up and my head is mostly filled with doubt.
I wish there was away I could carried these thoughts out,
Maybe put them in a recycle bin or send them away with a point of no return.
Or either put them in a harness and watch as they slowly burn.
Either way this doubt had taken up too much space and more than I can spare
I want to get rid of it but the thoughts wont allow the dare
I want to be happy but its hard with all the pain that surrounds me.
I feel like a cage bird dying to be free.
I don't know what awaits the other side but I no longer want to allow doubt to
rent space.
The doubt has taken over and I haven't slept in days

PLOTS

I know better days are coming least that's what I try to believe
I know people are plotting against me
But I cant focus on what they have up their sleeve.
Trying to channel my energy
To focus on the good don't know why when it comes to understandings
Things are often misconstrue and misunderstood
Searching for inner peace
While causing negative energy death
Trying to reevaluate some things and people
Had to start by looking out for self
Although they try to form
I cant allow them to have any room to prosper
I offer peace
Insecurity is being offered
Though I have no reason
No benefits to gain
I'm just trying to live my life
And my stability to maintain

HEAVY LIES THE HEAD PT.2

Heavy lies the head especially when you wear a crown.
Some people coming at me guess they trying to bring me down.
It's amazing how silence can make loudest sound.
Some people change on me when they thought they had me down.

Even when staring the unknown in its face.
I continue to wear a smile no feelings altering the smile on my face.

Heavy lies the head when u have alot on your mental.
It's funny how things seem so complicated yet it can be so simple.
Attacks coming form everywhere trying to destroy the temple.
Enemies trying to gain access but can't afford the rental.

Heavy lies the head of the person who has their own
Some people wonder how throughout the trails u remain strong.
Try to find forgiveness for your enemies when they try to do you wrong.
I'm protective of the energy, I allow into my home.

Heavy lies the head when you wear a crown.
Never allow the opinions of others penetrate and bring you down.
Don't entertain the circus just to see the clown.
Don't allow negativity be the reason u drown.
Remember heavy lies the head of the one who wears the crown.

VACANT SPOT

U say u want to be with me
And you have been checking me out for a while
U say u want to be the reason why
I wake up every morning with a smile
U say by want to restore what has been taken away
U say u will always protect me and make me feel safe
U say u want to take my child in and treat him as your own
U say u are ready to considered me
Your safe spot and home
U say u ready to occupy the space which was once null and void
U promise to love and protect me
My heart is yours and u won't destroy it

SCAR

If I put all the pieces on the table and show you all my cards, would you take
those pieces and see the beauty in my scars.
If I concealed a few pieces, and tuck them away.
Would you be more impressed with shallowness I chose to display.
Masked Identity

SORRY

I had accepted the last sorry I was ever going to take.
I don't want anymore sorry because of people choices and later calling it a mistake,
I don't want your sorry because the pile of sorry are stack to high.
Quite frankly they are holding me back I cant elevate and fly.
So keep your I am sorry please don't bring it to my door
I cant bear another sorry that apology is off tour.
You can take your sorry, I didn't mean to, my bad, and it wont happen again
And give it to someone else who is searching for an "I'm sorry friend".
I don't need it because I'm sorry keeps getting in my way.
Being I'm sorry has put a halt in my day.
I cant be productive I cant achieve any wins
If you stopping by to say I'm sorry go back and try again.
This round I'm packing up all the "I'm sorry" and the truth I'm about to dispel
I'm going to tell all the "I'm sorry" to have a nice trip to hell
I don't want your "I'm sorry" because it has expand my waist.
Don't come to me with an apology
I prefer not its taste.
So keep your apology
Don't knock or bring it to my door
I cant have another sorry
Greeting me at the door
And the next time instead of being sorry
Try being a better person and better you
Because I wont be sorry when I have to walk away from u.

HE SAID

He said he like having me in his life and he didn't want us to end
Even though he type up the words, he wasn't ready to hit send
He said he like the fact I was there and couldn't let me go
Even though he loved me, he love his freedom more
He said he liked me in his corner and all the advice I give
Even though he wasn't ready to commit, it didn't take away how he feel.
He said he likes me in his corner and he wasn't ready to let me out
When I came to him for advice that was his way of keeping others out
He said he invested too much in me to allow me to walk away
Even though another love may come, he will find a way to push them away.

FRIDAY NIGHTS

I always hated when Friday came because it would always be the same.
He would get drunk and beat me until I holler his name.
It's almost like he loved to see me black and blue
It's like everything I did, he found a way to criticize it to
How could the same man who said he love me
Abuse me with his words
Do some of the most unimaginable things
I ever heard
He took from me my joy, my spirit, and well being.
Why it always ended in blows whenever we were disagreeing
I loved him but all he did was take everything from me.
He took my pride, my joy, my ability to believe.
I loved him
Despite his faults. His lies and his deception.

LOVE NO MORE

I don't want to love anymore
I don't want to go through the heartaches and pain
I don't want to love anymore.
to the point I feel Insane

I don't want to feel used
Abuse
Or anything other than free
I don't have time to be held in captivity

Love can have you confuse
And caught up in a rut
People these days don't have your best interest
They are only interested in taking your stuff

Before I have anything else left to give
I rather live my life being free
Instead of traveling down hill

FIDDLE FOOTED

I wrestle with the thought over and over again
Tried telling myself, I can be your friend
After reevaluating all the things that transpire
I can't help but to feel I have did all that was required
I poured my all into you until there was nothing left
Thought if I gave my all to you then you would want me for yourself
I realize I could give and give but it was never enough for a soul that's empty
Cause I had nothing left and you benefit from plenty

Printed in the United States
by Baker & Taylor Publisher Services